Meet the Minibeasts

FUSION

Invertebrates in the WATER

by

Rebecca Phillips-Bartlett

BEARPORT
PUBLISHING

Minneapolis, Minnesota

Credits

All images are courtesy of Shutterstock.com, unless otherwise specified. With thanks to Getty Images, Thinkstock Photo, and iStockphoto. Recurring images – Guz Anna, Azamatovic, Net Vector, Tartila, Lana Sham, Rawpixel.com, Mari_Bryk, ebi_ko. Cover – Ivaschenko Roman, Henrik Larsson, Danut Vieru, Arton Kozyrev. 2–3 – clarst5. 4–5 – Brady Leavell, Marinodenisenko. 6–7 – Kiolk, natchapohn, olko1975. 8–9 – Ernie Cooper, Menno Pijpers, Gerald Robert Fischer. 10–11 – Hector Ruiz Villar, Martin Pelanek. 12–13 – Nature Picture Library, Vitalii Hulai. 14–15 – Carl Kristensen, Rostislav Stefanek. 16–17 – Erni, Przemyslaw Muszynski. 18–19 – Agami Photo Agency, Vitolga. 20–21 – R0macho, Vitalii Hulai. 22–23 – Haiduchyk Aliaksei, karelnoppe.

Bearport Publishing Company Product Development Team

Publisher: Jen Jenson; Director of Product Development: Spencer Brinker; Managing Editor: Allison Juda; Editor: Cole Nelson; Associate Editor: Naomi Reich; Associate Editor: Tiana Tran; Designer: Kim Jones; Designer: Kayla Eggert; Designer: Steve Scheluchin; Production Specialist: Owen Hamlin

Library of Congress Cataloging-in-Publication Data is available at www.loc.gov or upon request from the publisher.

ISBN: 979-8-89577-019-1 (hardcover)
ISBN: 979-8-89577-450-2 (paperback)
ISBN: 979-8-89577-136-5 (ebook)

For more information, write to Bearport Publishing, 5357 Penn Avenue South, Minneapolis, MN 55419.

CONTENTS

MINIBEASTS

IN THE WATER

Hello! My name is Frida Frog. I spend most of my time around my pond. I like to catch and eat **invertebrates**, such as **insects** and snails.

An invertebrate is an animal with no backbone.

I like calling these small and tasty animals minibeasts. My pond **habitat** is full of them. Let's dive in and meet some minibeasts!

Have you ever visited a pond before?

5

WATER STRIDERS

Water striders use their short front legs to catch food.

These amazing insects have tiny hairs on the bottom of their feet that push away water. This lets them walk on top of the water.

Water striders can feel when another insect has landed on the water's surface. Then, the water-walker begins to hunt!

FACT FILE

Size: Up to 0.75 inches (2 cm) long

Diet: Smaller insects

Habitat: Still and slow-moving water

BACKSWIMMERS

Backswimmers swim upside down just below the water's surface. They have hairs on their body that trap air. This lets them breathe underwater.

From above the water, the backswimmer's dark front blends in with the pond. When viewed from below, the backswimmer blends in with the bright sky. This helps **camouflage** the insect.

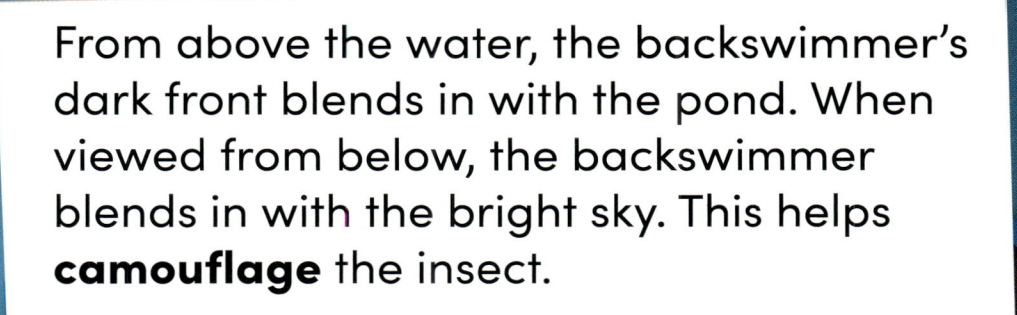

Where did this minibeast go?

FACT FILE

Size: Up to 0.5 in. (1.3 cm) long

Diet: Other insects, tadpoles, and small fish

Habitat: Ponds, lakes, and streams

DIVING BEETLES

Diving beetles are great swimmers. They spend most of their time underwater hunting for food. These insects often hunt animals bigger than they are.

Row of hairs

Diving beetles have rows of hairs on their back legs that help them swim underwater.

To get air underwater, the beetles stick their rear ends out of the water. This makes them look like they are diving. To breathe while they swim deeper in the pond, they hold air under their wing cases.

11

POND SNAILS

Snails help clean water by eating algae and dead plants.

You might have seen snails sliding around on the ground. But did you know some snails live underwater? Cone-shaped shells make pond snails easy to spot.

Pond snails have a strange way of moving around. They can crawl on the underside of the water's surface! These snails leave a trail of slime that helps them hang onto the surface and float upside down.

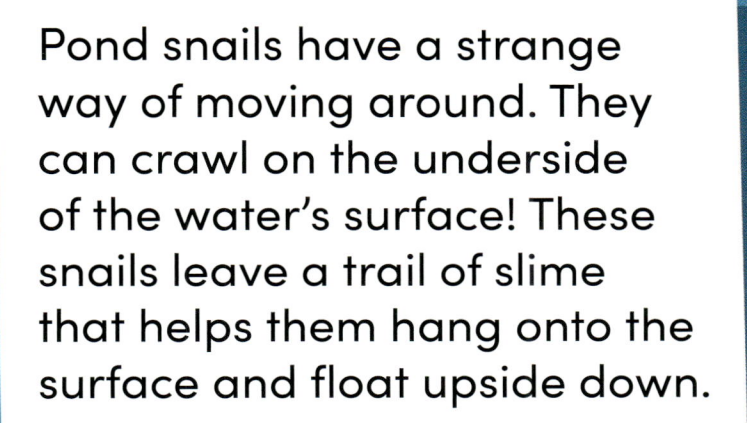

Snails are slimy, crunchy, and yummy!

FACT FILE

Size: Up to 4 in. (10 cm) long

Diet: Algae and plants

Habitat: Lakes, ponds, rivers, and streams

13

MAYFLIES

Mayflies spend their first two years living underwater as **nymphs**. These young insects burrow in the **silt** or cling to rocks underwater.

A mayfly nymph

These minibeasts take some digging to find!

14

After they grow up, adult mayflies leave the water and fly away to find a mate. But the adults live for only a few days. This is just long enough to lay eggs before they die.

An adult mayfly

Mayflies have been around for more than 300 million years.

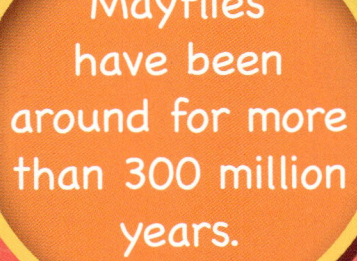

FACT FILE

Size: Up to 1 in. (2.5 cm) long

Diet: Nymphs eat algae, but adults do not eat at all!

Habitat: Ponds, lakes, and rivers

DRAGONFLIES

Like a mayfly, a dragonfly spends most of its life underwater as a nymph. It can be at this life stage for anywhere from two months to six years. The nymph spends most of its time hunting for food.

A dragonfly nymph

Dragonfly nymphs suck in water and spit it out to zoom around!

As a dragonfly nymph grows, it molts its skin as many as 14 times. When it is big enough, it leaves the water and molts one last time to change into an adult dragonfly.

An adult dragonfly

FACT FILE

Size: Up to 2.5 in. (6.5 cm) long

Diet: Other insects, small fish, and some crayfish

Habitat: Ponds, lakes, and rivers

WATER SCORPIONS

Water scorpions are minibeasts that hunt underwater. These insects use their tails to breathe while they look for food. They lift them above the water like little snorkels.

Tail

True scorpions use their tails to sting. Water scorpions do not have stingers.

Water scorpions are not very good swimmers. These minibeasts usually stay near the edges of ponds. They walk along the bottom and catch food with their large front legs.

Front legs

FACT FILE

Size: Up to 1.5 in. (3.5 cm) long

Diet: Tadpoles and small fish

Habitat: Pond edges

WHIRLIGIG BEETLES

These minibeasts are tasty but tiny!

Whirligig beetles are named because of the way they move. These adorable minibeasts spin and whirl around on top of the water in circle shapes.

Whirligig beetles have two sets of eyes. One pair looks up above the water. The other set looks underwater. This helps the insects spot **predators** coming from either direction.

These minibeasts use their flat back legs as paddles.

FACT FILE

Size: 0.75 in. (2 cm) long

Diet: Other small insects

Habitat: Ponds, lakes, and slow-moving rivers

21

SO MANY MINIBEASTS

A pond is home to so many amazing minibeasts. A lot of them help keep ponds and rivers healthy. Some eat dead plants. While others become food themselves.

A dragonfly

From the surface of a pond to its bottom, minibeasts find many places to make their homes underwater. Next time you are near the water, take a look. Can you see any minibeasts?

What is your favorite minibeast in the water?

GLOSSARY

camouflage to disguise oneself by blending into one's surroundings

habitat a place in nature where a plant or animal normally lives

insects small animals that have six legs and three main body parts

invertebrates animals without backbones

molt to shed an outer layer

nymphs the young of some insects, such as dragonflies

predators animals that hunt and eat other animals

silt small particles that settle at the bottom of a lake or river

INDEX